The Art of Love

By: Bruce Barry Jr.

This book is a work of poetry. Unless otherwise noted, the author and the publisher make no explicit guarantees as to the accuracy of the information contained in this book and in some cases; names of people places have been altered to protect their privacy.

© 2014For Bruce Barry Jr. & Published By Maximize Publishing Inc. Bronx New York, All Rights Reserved.

No part of this book may be reproduced, stored in a retrieval system, or transmitted by any means without the written permission of the author.

First Published for:
Maximize Publishing Inc.

ISBN-13:
978-0615979786.)

ISBN-10:
0615979785

The Art of Love

By: Bruce Barry Jr.

Phases

Unity Phase: Love shared in communion

Distance Phase: Love expressed in distance—physically, emotionally, or spiritually

Break-Up Phase: Determined to move forward…without you

Make-Up Phase: It. Is. Not. Over.

To My Readers

I am so grateful to you, my first readers. This really has been a long time in the making. I pray this touches you and is the start of a long healthy relationship between poet and listener. I give special thanks to those inspirational in my life, especially my mother who pushed to get my very first poem published at age 14. Special thanks to the Unity Fellowship of Christ Church NYC for allowing me space to grow and cultivate my talents. And to all my fellow poets and writers out there—keep writing, keep imagining, and keep creating!

Bruce Barry Jr.

Special Thanks:

Anthony London, for being a friend and a support

Deborah McKeever, for believing in me

Ms. Sampson, one of my grade school teachers wherever she may be, for seeing my potential

The late Mabel Barry, my grandmother, for always pushing me forward

Unity Phase

It's beautiful when we're together. It's so beautiful when we're together...

The Whispers In The Morning

You came from out of nowhere

A reminder of my dreams

A blessing from the angels

A life of love decreed.

I have been liberated—your love has set me free

It has made a way ages ago for the Lord to bless me

The whispers in the morning is what you have given me

The whispers in the morning you saying you love me

The whispers in the morning is what I need

Your voice lingering on the bed sheets

Speaking softly in love

Telling my how treasured I am

How valued I am

And I want nothing more than to whisper in return

The same affirmations and praises

To tell you how incredible you are

How much I want these whispers—this morning to never end

I could lay here with you for eternity

And we would dream our dreams and speak only of love

Oh how I am inspired by your determination

To love and to be loved

To be joyous and give joy

To touch and be touched

For the sweet love we make in every passing moment I am grateful

Grateful for all these moments

For all these whispers …

In the morning

You

My eyes have beheld many treasures

I've seen so many things in my lifetime

But now I see something I've never seen before

I've never seen anyone like you

Through many times and many changes—and how life rearranges

There has been none like you

You are the center of my heart

You are the apple of my eye

You are my prize from heaven

I love you

So let's stay together and grow

Let's stay together and show

Show the world our love

This gift from above

You have captivated me

Now the time is come for our union to grow

We're on this journey together

We're in God's hands

Our love is according to his plan and will

It's our time and you?

You are my love

You are my treasure

And we will go in peace

For the sake of love

And the sake of joy

We will be whole

We will be complete

And I couldn't be happier with the way things are

And it's all because of that angel that blessed me

All because of the radiant smile that I have found

All because of that mouth-watering passion

It is all because of you

You…

Your love

Words cannot express the depth of your love

Wisdom cannot capture it in thought

It cannot be defined simply

Your love is divine

Your love is greater than I

Your love takes me high

I could never have enough

It blesses me—it assures me

Your love sets me free

I've tried to understand why

I wanted to know how I could deserve this

This love, this light you have bestowed upon me

But it cannot be found

Your love floors me

Takes my every breath away, yet still gives me new life every moment

Oh my God…how I love you

How I love your love

How I love your love!

I could never be tired of your touch,

Embrace me always

Kiss me always

Love me always

And I'll be ever careful, to care for your love

And let it not return void

Oh…your love

Oh! Your love…

I Never Thought

I never thought that I would be the one to fall in love

I never thought that I'd be sitting here thinking of you

Because I was naïve, I was so silly

I kept hiding my emotions

Who would have guessed we'd be together

It seems as though I really let myself go

I'll never let you go—

No baby, no

I will never let you shed a tear

I am coming undone with every day I don't hear your voice

You're so perfect in my eyes and could do no wrong

The image of innocence and purity

When I'm with you it's like a higher power is blessing me

You are so beautiful

And it's like I met you yesterday… we are so young into the relationship

Already I think I can love you forever

You are

That ray of hope, my shining light

I never thought that I was the kind to fall in love

I never thought we'd be in love

I never thought…

My love

My love it's so amazing how time has passed us by

My love we keep on growing and changing by and by

My love you've been my shelter

A refuge from the storm

And now it's time to make love,

Create love and make it strong

I will never forget our value

I will never do you harm

I will always keep reaching for you

When I'm weak and when I'm strong

And when life ends and I am called home

To meet the savior Lord

I will speak of love that only

Could be born from his own

<u>Carry Me</u>

The one to carry me

To hold the weight of my heart

His hands tight with the grips of life

His shoulders broadened by his experiences

His strength is uncanny

And his charm unmatched

What a wonder to behold

What a way to be held

Caressed by this enormous force of love

Embraced with the width of desire

How he desires to touch every inch of my surfaces

And explore deep inside my everything

Come to me and carry me off to be made in love

Strip me of these barriers

Carry me to the place of nakedness

Then give me rapture with your touch, your kiss, and your course

I am an open vessel waiting to be lifted

Carry me to the closed doors

And pull out your secret positions

Place your desires inside of my waiting temple

And I'll receive you

Engulf you and intake your every particle

Carry me to that place

The place where no one matters but the two of us

You carrying me

Hmm… ecstasy

Beautiful

How the light dances in your eye

How the music sways your shoulders

How the fragrant smell of your body welcomes me

It diminishes my fear

It maxes out my security

It's beautiful when we're together

It's so beautiful when we're together

My every worry is melted in your kiss

Everywhere your hands rest I am healed of all anxiety

How safe I am with you

How beautiful you are—and radiant, and powerful, and strong, and gracious

Beautiful—the entirety of your being

Encompassing all your attributes, your desires and

Longing to share them with me and me in love alone

How beautiful a love I have never known

I wonder on it

I respect it—but do not understand it

How could you have so much reverence?

So much patience and virtue

Why would you love someone like me?

With my stains and complexities

And then it became clear to me

Why you sacrificed for me

Why you so adherently refused to give up on me

I never saw why you valued me—

I never saw why I should value myself

And then it became clear

You saw me—even before I saw me

And when you saw me you had these same feelings

You thought that I—even I was beautiful

Me? I?

I was beautiful

I had my own allure to you

I had my own chemistry

You saw me and loved it

You saw me and loved me

How confused and misguided I was

And it was so beautiful together

We we're so beautiful together

How God has dealt me a hand of Favor!

Favor

Favor…

Beauty…

What we are together

Beauty

May it never end.

Distance Phase

How much I miss just being able to see you on the other side of the room

Missing You

I think about the time we shared together

Those first tender moments

And I say to myself "wow, love is here"

And we've grown and shown one another that we care

But in lies one clause

We are apart and the distance feels like what it is

Miles of separation

Acres of space between you and I

But I love you ever stronger

Ever boldly

I hold up the bloodstained banner of my heart

And continue to press forward

But in the crevices of my heart I ache

To feel your touch

And experience your presence

My being wants nothing more than to be unified in body and spirit

How I wish we were together in this moment

All of our passions and our desires

All of our yearnings

All of our beings

Present in one space and time

The joy it would be to make love with you

The joy it would be to be present with you

I want to go to that place

I want to hold you in my arms

Instead of this sweet lingering suffering I must endure

I hold my head high and hold things together

But the reality is I need my man

And I need him here with me

I'm missing you…

Heart Beat Again

When I see you—my heart beats again

When I need you—my heart beats again

And when I'm with you

My heart beats again

Surely I need you to survive

Help my heart beat again

Make my heart beat again

It's cold now, I need you next to me

I'm growing old now

No play time left for me

I need you there to show you care

I need you tenderly

My heart, it cannot live without your love

I'm here now waiting for your love

Draw near now

We'll share an endless love

I need you there, to show you care

This time away from you prolongs a pointless suffering

When we both know we'll be better together

So make up your mind and pack up your things

And move right back into my life

I'm waiting for my resuscitation

I need my heart to beat again

And you hold the key to my vitality

Make my heart beat again

Help my heart beat again…

The Beauty Dimension

The first look captivated—caught my attention

His face, glowing with some Godly illustrious light

I wondered what celestial being I had encountered

His eyes…such that had a soft intensity

They radiated—they invited—they mesmerized

I fell in love—no into infatuation

No—into the beauty dimension

To touch his countenance was unspeakable

But to sit and behold his wonder was glorious

Will I ever see him again?

Only time knows

But his beauty—it shall remain in its luster

I'll remember him forever more

And I will see him again

He'll be visiting my dreams while I lie in wait

Maybe this one sweet time he'll notice me—

By God acknowledge me!

Oh to be welcomed into his dominion

His beauty dimension

What joyous rapturous music we would make together

The heavens would never cease their singing

For he was beautiful…my God he was so beautiful

And he was pleasant, and he was fair, and he was gorgeous

But most of all he was oh, so beautiful

In that moment as my dimension crossed his own

For one moment I loved him

I lived him

Needed him

So many opportunities where in his glance

And his smile was a thousand memories

And oh my God he was beautiful

His beauty dimension has captured me

And I cannot escape this sweet entanglement

It makes me believe again

In love and laughter and fantasy

This poem is endless

Its depth uncharted because—

Just because oh my God he was beautiful

He is beautiful

He is beautiful

He is so very beautiful

I love his presence

I love his visage

I love his beauty dimension

Saturation

There is dampness my spirit

Moisture that leaves me cold and aimless

It is the residue of my tears

My tears for love defeated

And heartache repeated

Once again I spilled my heart to the one who I thought would love me

But yet again the awkward return leaves me staunched

My palms sweaty and head lightened

Like that teenage boy with the tawdry love letter tucked into his back pocket

I stood there like a foolish child expecting to be showered with your love

I was waiting for saturation

But all I found was the wetness of my tears

And you in the arms of another

You told me we could never be

That you were happy where you were

And I felt insignificant for waiting so long to tell you

To show you my love

I sat in waiting in my own corner

Pining for you, praying for you

But never courageous enough to make my move

Never strong enough to utter a word

I watched him take your hand and never detested

How could I expect to be rewarded after my silent suppression?

I wanted you to shower me with your love

But all I got was this dampness

This saturation

The saturation of my tears

Blushing

He caught me on a subway train… with such a quick glance

I could have almost missed him

Tall and radiant, fragrant and enticing

He was so richly organized from head to toe

I had to give myself a once over—just to be sure

Just to be sure he could be talking to me

Uttering those sweet words that have never departed

But left me… blushing

Our interaction was brief—momentary

None the like that happens by happenstance

Nor the kind geared in the direction of feeding only my fleshly desires

No… he was the kind of man that fed my spirit

A sprite of pure nature

A glimpse of an eternity in love

He spoke to me and,

I had to give myself a once over—just to be sure

Just to be sure he could be talking to me

Uttering those sweet words that have never departed

But left me... blushing

He said to me that I had beauty

He said to me that I had quality

He said to me that I had spirit

He admired my attributes

And I admired his honesty

His openness and his courage

He actually cared, actually meant what he said

He wasn't tied to the outcome, nor did he have more motives than apparent

And he made his way on to his destination leaving me breathless

I had to give myself a once over—just to be sure

Just to be sure he could be talking to me

Uttering those sweet words that have never departed

But left me… blushing

Shades of Blue

I don't know why this color offends me

Why every time I see it, I cringe

My tears hide for no one

My pain finds no release

I can't help but remember our love

In these rich shades and tinted hues

Our love that was so strong

Our love that I thought was permanent

How mistaken I was

How wrongly I have behaved

How judgmental I've been

But now as usual I return to my better senses

Defeated. Tired. Repenting. And ashamed

You've had your share of my mistakes

And the taste of my love has probably grown stale on your lips

Yet still I remain in my ignorance

Still I see only my wants and my needs

My self-centeredness truly wins out

As my ego sets out to destroy itself

My eye catches this tone

Yet again this blue daze shocks my heart into fertile submission

And I couldn't cry hard enough or loud enough for the inequities on my part

These shades of blue keep me haunted and undecided, questioning my every move—

Questioning my every love

Because I know I love you— so why?

Why didn't I stay?

Why didn't I forgive you?

When you so utterly desired me

When you so openly revealed the truth

While I felt compelled to keep my secrets and manipulate for my own interests

I wonder again if I really know what love is—

If I'm really ready to experience that

And I see you over there smiling

Smiling in that blue ensemble

And I'm burning here in my own self-inflicted loneliness

And you are unaware of how much I desire you

How much I miss just being able to see you on the other side of the room

And I …

And I remember these shades of blue

Blue really was our color wasn't it?

Distance

Distance…separation

Space…

The words that could not even fully envelope the course of what I am going through

There is so much love in my heart that goes by your blind eye time and time again

You can't see my yearnings, my desires

To touch and kiss your face

Your spirit is otherwise placed

Your heart is otherwise concerned

And your mind?

Well it's on a different page

What a waste of time this is

Me sitting here loving you and you can't even understand the value of my presence

I doubt you even know what love—true love is

And it makes me wonder

Am I the problem?

Am I the one who doesn't understand?

And my prayers for clarity couldn't ring loud enough in my heart

I try desperately to fill the void you left with your ignorance

But nothing suffices

Nothing is ever enough

But this distance is not my imagination,

This space is not a formality

We truly aren't on the same wavelength

But it makes me pursue you even more

Love you more ferociously

What is it with us as lovers always wanting what we cannot and should not have?

Will we ever learn?

Will I ever learn to let go of the meaningless and detrimental?

Will this pain-bearing love ever end?

Or will I continue to play the victim and not learn the value of my own love?

The value of my own peace

I must find my joy again

I must find myself again

You see in this distance—

I have distanced myself from what is most important

Me...

The distance is in me

From me

I've distanced myself from my own existence and become consumed with you

I can't let these miles separate me for much longer

I must rediscover what it's like

What it's like not to be distanced

Distanced from me

Break-Up Phase

You will be in my heart but It's done and I'm moving on now...

A Part of Me

When you left I thought I would die

I just cried and cried and cried

Because you're a part of me

When you are on my mind—

I think of the love we shared, it was so sweet

I can remember the sound of your voice

And I had no choice—I had to follow you

Hold on to me, I can't stay forever

But I can make our time worth it—

Worth risking it all

And I'll force myself not to cry when you leave me

And then I'll wait—time always kills the pain

Almost always…

Maybe always…

I…

I'll love for you on the other side

Let us turn forever, love is not free

You are a part of me—it's too plain to see

I love you and you love me but…

Don't you know I gotta move on?

I'm never coming back home…

Maybe I…

Anything is possible

My Love Immortal

I'm so tired of reality, facing the facts and the truth

I know our time is limited the days shorter as they go

I want you know that I love you

My love is immortal for you

At night I dream about a time when you held me close

And I'd wake and cry knowing that you'll soon be gone

The clouds fade into oblivion as my emotions skyrocket

Please, please baby please don't go I love you so much

But I know you have to… still please know

My love is immortal for you

As you wipe my tears and kiss my sorrow away I wish—

Wish you could be there to stay

I love you now and will always love you

The sound of the voice of you just drove me to pure insanity

But still you leave me

I wish things weren't so difficult—

I wish this could last forever, I...

I don't know what else to say but I love you baby

So, so much

From the first time I saw you I was captivated, remember?

My love is immortal for you

Please wipe my tears one last time

Tell me you love me

Because this is goodbye "I love you"

And then suddenly I know this is reality

So I'm here without you... only me

Forget Me

Dawdling in the aspects of life

Face against the truth

Watching the sky's tears

Figuring out a title for every storm

Will not these tears be heard?

Don't you see I am waiting for you?

For your life to be a part of mine

OWN me!

Did you forget about me?

I, who have stood by your side, even when you faced torture and torment,

I who have loved you for who you are

I who have held your hand

I who was your eyes when you could not see

And I who was your ears when you could not hear

Me! How dare you forget me!

The life, the tourniquet—I am bound by what you did

Never escaping your judgment…

Captivating yet dangerous

Jeopardizing my everything, everything that is you

I cannot ask to be forgiven

But I have one request

Don't you ever forget me…

If I Could

If I could have one wish and was on my death bed

I'd have looked that wish in the eye and would have said

One last time I want the one I love

One last kiss from the one I love

If I could I would wish for you my hope, my life

Nothing but little strands of light

And then you would come with my heart in your hands

And you'd cry and beg me not to go but somehow some way, I go

My love for you goes beyond what love can say

I'll follow you anywhere each and every day

To the ether or to perdition

That is our choice

Yet I love you so much I don't even have a voice

My love burns me in the darkest hours of night

And I know you'll be with me

So I have no fright and I live

Even though you're gone I have to move on

I will love you forever

I will love you for eternity

I will lover you to infinity

I will love you forever to be…

If I could I would, and I will! Love you forever, infinity, and eternity

Disappointed

I'm disappointed—not so much in you

I guess I finally had to see what the world was like

I had my hopes and I had my dreams

Sweetened with my childlike innocence

I'm not crying cause you hurt me

I'm crying because I didn't know I could hurt

I'm not lying, I'm just trying

To deal with my disappointment

In the world

I'm growing up now—

No more fairy tales

I see now that there's more than clouds and roses

I actually thought that love played fair

Truth is love plays dirty and likes to scare

It's okay that you hurt me

I really don't judge you at all

I actually took what was worth me

And I gave it all away

I forgot the world was cold

The world was cold

I can't give my heart to anyone with a line and a smile

I really have to remember the world is cold

So find someone worth while

Worthwhile

I'm not crying cause you hurt me

I'm crying because I didn't know I could hurt

I'm not lying—I'm just trying

To deal with my disappointment

In the world…

Why Won't You Hold Me

I think, I feel

I cry, I sigh

Why won't you hold me?

And love me like you did before…when we were young

I remember those sweet days

When we forgave each other and love was made to each other

Why won't you hold me?

The love and passion we shared burned holes in our sheets

The fire we started raged till the sun rose

And still then burned ever more

But that love is gone

Those tender caresses are only memories

And those fire filled nights have be extinguished with icy animosity

And the cold shoulder rests upon our every thought and interaction

And "I love you" is the furthest thing from our tongues

I keep wondering…

Why won't you hold me?

I realize now that what's done is done

I can't hold on to those plighted dreams and the past

I can't hold on to the plundered fate of our love

I see now it's over…

I understand why you won't hold me

Because really, it's time to move on

Moving On

I remember the day we first met

There was love in the air and when we felt it we thought it would last forever

We thought that we had it all planned

All the years and the times to come that we said we were going to be together

But I think we both knew that what we had would break

No matter how hard we could try

And I felt my heart splitting when we met the day

So I kissed you goodbye

And I said please don't cry

You will be in my heart

But it's done and I'm moving on

And you gave me your words

And yes they were heard

You will be in my heart

But it's done and I'm moving on

It's time to move on without an us here and now

There were moments we cherished

And the times we let go

We've influenced so much—maybe we'll never know

There is so much out there for us

We've got to go explore and know

So I'll kiss you goodbye

And I'll say please don't cry

You will be in my heart

But it's done and I'm moving on

And you'll give me your words

Those words will be heard

You will be in my heart

But it's done and I'm moving on

I'm afraid we must part

For its done and I'm moving on

You will be in my heart

But it's done and I'm moving on now!

I'm missing you all over again

And I told myself be stronger

That's the way it has to be between us now

Then again some days I don't feel you at all

And I know by then its time and that I have to move on with my future

But I stopped crying for us far too long ago

To turn around and start all over now

You need to understand me…I'm just trying to let you go

It's time to move on

My forgiveness is done

We've found resolution

You will be in my heart

But it's done and I'm moving on now

And you gave me more words

And still they were heard

You will be in my heart

But it's done and I'm moving on

We must be apart

For its done and I'm moving on

You will stay in my heart

But it's done and I'm moving on now!

So I kissed you goodbye

And I said please don't cry

And you gave me your words

And then I…

Make-Up Phase

Can we go back to the way things, they used to be? You and me, you and me

Why Won't You Hold Me (Reprise)

Why won't the love we had rekindle?

Why won't the passion outweigh the pain?

Why can't we fall in love again?

Why can't we start the rain?

And why, why won't you hold me?

My love has never burned brighter

My faith—never stronger

I believe in you—I've given my all just to have this moment with you

And all you do is stand there

Staring blankly at me

Don't you know love when you see it?

Why won't you hold me?

Don't you recognize this golden opportunity?

Believe in me—believe in us

And come with me one more time

This time we'll make it work

This time we'll make it last—

Make it count

Still you stand there

Why won't you hold me?

Damn all the odds!

Forget the struggles!

This is the time to start fresh don't you see all our goals on the horizon?

Our dreams recognized together

Yes!

We can make it this time

Yes!

Stop standing there looking at me!

Why won't you hold me?

I know you love me!

I know you feel me!

I know you see my every tear!

Why won't you—

Okay, I see now

Maybe I've made my point

I'll stop talking now and start acting

Boy!

Get over here and let me hold you…

You and Me

So much time has gone by

Since we last shared an embrace

Since we last even spoke of love

I wonder where you are constantly

And it's frightening to know

That as I lay here pondering your everything in the deepest sorrow

You are somewhere actually living

Breathing and smiling

And I wonder

Do you ever think about me anymore?

I know I said let's just be friends

But do you wish there was more

Can we go back to the way things they used to be?

You and me

You and me

I wonder what really happened between us

The real unspoken words beyond our pointless arguments

And I feel like somehow I'm responsible

I pushed you away and was closed, not open—

I forced you into corners

Gave you ultimatums

My childish ways!

But now it's all clear to me

All I want to do is apologize

Make things right between us again

And I see that glimmer in your eye

And it makes me wonder

Do you ever think about me anymore?

I know I said let's just be friends

But do you wish there was more

Can we go back to the way things they used to be?

You and me

You and me

You... and me

Again

Here we go again

Falling in love

I swore I'd never see you again

Swore I'd never need your touch

But look at me—like a spoiled child throwing a tantrum

I desire you—want and need you right now

Again

You look at me, that melts all my anger—

Everything you did wrong—

Every mistake you made

Everything you said

Melted because

Again I find myself in love with you

I've been ignoring all the bruises we left on each other

But now in this moment we're healing our open wounds

Restoring our trust in one another

Making us work again

Again

I never thought I'd crave you like this

That we'd want each other so fervently

But here we are again

Again

Sweet communion

Sweet reunion

Giving our all in this try

Giving everything we have in order to make our hearts mend

And blend this time

Again

This will be the final try this time

We'll defy perdition and survive

We'll survive

Because we're stronger than before

Wiser and so much more

Prepared to give all of what's in store

Nay Sayers can't stop us

Because our love is impenetrable

Again

<u>We Cannot Forget</u>

They tell us both to move on

To let the other go

But really how can we leave?

How can we stop connecting?

How can we stop loving?

With this passion that burns through the night

And is the envy of the sun

How can we simply move on?

No!

We can't forget

When the love making brings us to tears

We can't forget

After all of these years

We can't forget

Though it's sometimes sealed with pain

We cannot forget!

So touch me!

Would it be easier to lay there alone?

Would it suit you more to never kiss these lips again?

These lips that have been declared your own time and time again

This body that is the land of your permanent adventure

Love me!

Don't leave me alone here in this place

What do I have to offer the world but to be your perfect lover?

Do you not remember the nights of endless fire?

Do you not recall the sheets drowning in our love?

I see the flames in your soul and I know you remember

No!

We can't forget

The yearnings and desire

We can't forget

The bedroom set afire

We can't forget

A timeless love

We Cannot Forget!

Remove this absence

Restore our union

Feel me! Want my everything!

I am so willing to give

Forsake me not for the past is a marker for us to learn

And though we must let go to move forward

Though we must forget those former things

Though that chapter is now complete

There is one thing for certain

No matter how much they try to tear us apart

We never will…simply because

We cannot forget!

The Phoenix Complex

We've been here before…

Eternity has come and gone

We lived in peace for so long

But then near then end flames ensued

We argued. We shouted. We accused. We blamed. We cursed.

Then, we burst

Burst into flames

And now we lay in the ashes yet again

But this place is all too familiar

This insipid cat and mouse game we play isn't old to us

We prosper. We fail. We reconsider. We re-unite.

And as we lay here in ashes as the flames subside this one thing is discovered

We're living in the phoenix complex

Ages pass us by or so it seems

And our love lives!

It experiences, it grows!

And yet, it ages and the life of love itself comes to a screeching halt

The age has paid its toll

And we burst into funeral fire

And everything we knew burns away

Every sweet word dies and lies in ruin

But we never stay there

We never let it ruin the possibility of a bright and prosperous future

And like the phoenix we rise from the funeral pyre

And young in love again we realize immortality

Our love will never cease to exist

I don't care how many times we reject it

I don't care how many time we have to burn all of our possessions

I will never leave us there in the end

I will never, not rise from those ashes and start all over

The love we share is worth dying a thousand deaths just for the opportunity to rise again

With new understanding

With new hope

With new dreams

And opened eyes

And immortality shall be our prize

This is us

This is who we are and what we want to be

This is the phoenix complex

Recompense For The Lonely

I see you over there

In your fainted stare

And I can honestly say I'm proud to tell you

"I told you so"

You think you can hide your true feelings from me

But I can see that your heart is drying up from lack of nourishment

Didn't I tell you, that you would miss me?

Did I not say that you would come crawling back?

I told you, you were making a mistake when you left

I begged you not to leave me—I put away my pride and begged

Yet you swore you were through

And that you would never need me again

How foolish your assumptions were

And to think you were so full of yourself

So full of arrogance and malice

Yet here you stand

With eyes screaming for recompense for the lonely

What would I be to give into that look?

That look…

That look that always shatters every defense I ever fabricate

That look that illuminates that pathway to your heart

That look that destroys my ability to breathe

That kind of love is the love you walked away from

And how dare you come back to me now bashful and afraid

Step up to me!

Make me see that it is you that I want

Make me!

Make me give you recompense for the lonely

Make my head spin and my breath short

I'll forget everything else in that moment

Tearing at my clothes and tugging at my hair

Because the sight of you so far away from me

Burns my body with a flame only you ignite and only you can douse

Wait....

It's me who was the lonely one wasn't it?

<u>Enough</u>

We've fought enough

There are no more names to call each other

No more lies to reveal

No more secrets to tell

Enough is enough

No more fighting

No more disagreeing

I know you said you needed space

But you see, you left my soul in this barren place

And I can't seem to live without you

I can't make it anymore

So I have no choice

I have to make things right

I have to repair what I destroyed for the sake of my heart

And for the sake of our love

I need you to hear me like you've never heard me before

What is left to fight about?

You see... I know you love me

And dammit I won't let that die

I won't let you turn away from me

I love you with so much of me

It's hard to find some of me left for myself

I won't bicker with you anymore

I won't play the waiting game

Trying to see if you leave or stay

If you'll love or stray

I can't play these dangerous games anymore

Too much is at stake

And my heart is on the line

Our lives are on the line

We mean too much to each other, and carry too much power

How is it that just the wrong look from you can destroy me?

Just one word off center shrinks my entire being

How can my actions incite such anger and fury from you?

Why do we have such power and abuse it

Abuse each other

Enough

I think it's time we bury the past

And stop inflicting this senseless dissonance

What purpose would it serve us to live out our lives separately

If we destroy our hearts and ruin ourselves for love

Enough is truly enough

It's time to use this power, this energy, to encourage each other

And to build one another up

If you say you love me act upon it

I'll show you this one last time how much you mean to me

This one last time what love truly looks like

And we won't fail—if we've truly had enough

So come on, let's do this

For the sake of all the good that's in store

For me and for you

For all that we can do together

For our potential

Love me one last time

And I'll love you everlastingly

Here we go again

I guess this is the part that we could never do…Enough

About The Author

Bruce Barry Jr was born to Carol Barry and Bruce Barry Sr. Poetry has been his venue for self-expression and creativity from a very young age, with hundreds of poems ranging from love and relationship to social justice, racism, spirituality and mysticism. In his early life he was a published poet who has work in the books "A Surrender to The Moon" and "Poetry Slam Book: New York's Best Poets." Bruce has a love for all of creative expression and expresses himself in any form possible. Poetry, however, was his first love. He is a young aspiring author with deep insight and profound wisdom to offer unparalleled with his natural age.

This Work of Poetry Was Published By

415-779-6297 Or MaximizePublishingInc@gmail.com

www.ingramcontent.com/pod-product-compliance
Lightning Source LLC
Chambersburg PA
CBHW051948160426
43198CB00013B/2351